Marine Mammals

DOLPHINS

ZELDA KING

PowerKiDS press.
New York

Published in 2012 by The Rosen Publishing Group, Inc.
29 East 21st Street, New York, NY 10010

First Edition

Editor: Joanne Randolph
Book Design: Julio Gil

Photo Credits: Cover Mike Hill/Getty Images; pp. 4, 5, 6 (top, bottom), 7, 8 (top, bottom), 9, 10, 11, 12, 13, 14–15, 18–19, 22 Shutterstock.com; p. 16 Jeff Rotman/The Image Bank/Getty Images; p. 17 Alexander Safonov/Flickr/Getty Images; p. 20 Stuart Westmorland/Stone/Getty Images; p. 21 Stuart Westmorland/The Image Bank/Getty Images.

Library of Congress Cataloging-in-Publication Data

King, Zelda.
 Dolphins / by Zelda King. — 1st ed.
     p. cm. — (Marine mammals)
 Includes index.
 ISBN 978-1-4488-5003-7 (library binding) — ISBN 978-1-4488-5137-9 (pbk.) —
ISBN 978-1-4488-5138-6 (6-pack)
 1. Dolphins—Juvenile literature. I. Title.
 QL737.C432K57 2012
 599.53—dc22

                                        2010048458

Manufactured in the United States of America

CPSIA Compliance Information: Batch #WS11PK: For Further Information contact Rosen Publishing, New York, New York at 1-800-237-9932

CONTENTS

Dolphins Are Dandy

Have you ever seen a dolphin? Almost everyone has. These **marine** animals have starred in TV shows and movies. Dolphins are also favorite **performers** in shows at zoos and aquariums. They are smart **mammals** that like to jump and play. As a result, they can be trained to do tricks.

Most dolphins in shows are bottlenose dolphins. They do well in shows because they seem to enjoy being around people. They

Wild bottlenose dolphins such as these can live up to 30 years.

also appear happy all the time. The shape of the bottlenose dolphin's mouth makes it look like it is always smiling!

Dolphins interest people a great deal. Many people visit aquariums every year to see dolphins up close.

You can find dolphins in oceans around the world. Dolphins live in the Atlantic Ocean, the Pacific Ocean, and the Indian Ocean. They live in almost all parts of these oceans, from the far north to the far south. Dolphins also live in the Mediterranean Sea, the Red Sea, and the Black Sea.

Above: Not all dolphins live in the ocean. There are five species of dolphins that live in rivers, including the pink boto, or Amazon River dolphin. *Right*: This dolphin swims in the ocean off the coast of Alabama.

This dolphin makes its home in warm waters near a coral reef. Dolphins that live in warm water have less blubber, or fat, than those that live in colder water.

Dolphins have **adapted** to all sorts of ocean settings. Some live near the shore, where the water is not too deep. Others live far out in the ocean. Many dolphins like to live in warm water. Others favor cold water.

Different Sorts of Dolphins

When you picture dolphins, you likely picture bottlenose dolphins. They are the most famous kind of dolphin. However, they are not the only type of dolphin. There are about 35 kinds of dolphins in the world.

Bottlenose dolphins can be up to 14 feet (4 m) long and weigh more than 1,000 pounds (450 kg).

Above: Orcas hunt for fish, seals, sharks, and even whales in oceans around the world. *Right*: Dusky dolphins live off the coasts of South America, southwestern Africa, southern Australia, New Zealand, and a few islands.

Bottlenose dolphins look friendly, but they are one of the top predators in the ocean.

Some dolphins are smaller. The two largest dolphins are commonly called whales. They are the pilot whale and the killer whale, or orca. The orca is the biggest. It can be up to 32 feet (10 m) long and weigh 18,000 pounds (8,200 kg)!

What type of body does an ocean animal need for swimming? It needs a body that can move quickly and easily through water, of course. That is exactly the kind of body a dolphin has. Its smooth skin has no hair. It swims using two powerful **flippers** and strong tail fins, called **flukes**. A fin on the dolphin's back helps it stay straight in the water.

Dolphins' flukes are powerful. They use them to move quickly through the water and even to jump high above the water.

Dolphins are commonly gray, although river dolphins may be more colorful. Under the dolphin's skin is fat called **blubber** that helps it stay warm. It breathes through a **blowhole** on top of its head.

The blowhole on top of a dolphin's head lets air in when it comes to the top. It seals tightly shut while the dolphin is underwater, though.

A Mammal Not a Fish

Dolphins live in water and look much like fish. What makes them mammals then? The blowhole is one clue. Do you know what it is for? The blowhole is for breathing air, just like your nose and mouth. A dolphin cannot breathe underwater. In fact, it closes its blowhole when it is underwater. It must come up and raise its blowhole above the water to breathe. A fish, however, can breathe only underwater. It cannot breathe air.

Bottlenose dolphins can hold their breath for about 7 minutes before coming up to breathe. Most people can hold their breath for only 2 minutes.

Like all mammals, dolphins are **warm-blooded** and have a backbone. Also like other mammals, mother dolphins feed milk to their young.

Mammals generally care for their young for a period of time. This mother spinner dolphin is swimming with two young dolphins.

13

The smile that bottlenose dolphins always seem to have hides a lot of sharp teeth. They have about 100 teeth. That is about three times as many teeth as a grown person has! Most types of dolphins have a lot of teeth. Some kinds have more than 200.

The teeth in a person's mouth are different shapes and sizes. Some are for biting and some are for chewing. All of a dolphin's teeth are sharp and cone shaped. Dolphins use their teeth to grab their food but not to chew it. Dolphins swallow their food whole!

Dolphins' teeth are just right for holding on to slippery fish. If dolphins chewed their food, they would have some flat teeth for crushing or grinding.

A Dolphin's Dinner

With all those sharp teeth, what kind of food do dolphins catch? They eat mostly fish and squid. Squid are ocean animals that are somewhat like octopuses. Some dolphins also eat other animals, such as shrimp.

Do you know how dolphins find their food? They use a system called **echolocation**. They make clicking sounds. The large bumps of fat on their heads, called melons, direct the sounds into the water.

This dolphin is eating an octopus it has found on the seafloor.

When the sounds strike an object, they bounce back as **echoes**. The echoes tell dolphins where objects are, what direction they are moving, and how fast they are moving.

Dolphins often work together to herd fish into one place. This makes it easier for dolphins to catch and eat a greater number of fish.

Pals in the Pod

Dolphins generally live in groups, called pods. Pods may be small or huge. There are three basic kinds. Mothers and their young form one type. When youngsters are three to six years old, they group together in **juvenile** pods. Adult males move between pods, swim alone, or form a close friendship with another adult male.

Pod members work together when hunting for food. They have also been known to help sick or hurt dolphins.

Both young and old dolphins like to play. They chase each other and toss objects around. Sometimes they swim, roll, and jump out of the water together!

Did You Know?

Dolphins talk to each other using whistles. They whistle to keep in touch with their pod members or to greet another pod. Each dolphin has its own special whistle.

Spinner dolphins sometimes swim in huge pods of thousands of dolphins. They are named for the way they make spinning jumps out of the water.

19

The Life of a Dolphin

A mother dolphin carries her baby inside her body for about a year. Another female dolphin, called an auntie, helps with the birth. The auntie helps the newborn rise to take its first breath.

The baby stays with its mother for three to six years. During this time, it learns many things, including the best way to breathe and how to use echolocation.

When the youngster is ready, it leaves to join a

Here a mother and auntie bottlenose dolphin swim with a calf.

juvenile pod. There it learns much about how to act with other dolphins. When it is about 10 years old, it is ready to **mate** and have its own baby!

This spinner dolphin sticks close to its calf as they head to the top of the water for a breath.

Dolphin Dangers

Wild dolphins do not have many enemies. Sharks and killer whales may hunt them, but dolphins are not an easy meal. Just like people, dolphins can become ill and die. Sometimes large groups of healthy dolphins **strand** themselves on beaches and die. Scientists are not certain why.

People present the biggest danger to dolphins. In some places, people hunt them. Sometimes dolphins get trapped in fishing nets and drown. People have destroyed the places some kinds of dolphins live. People have also caused ocean **pollution**, which can sicken and kill dolphins. Each of us needs to work to keep these wild and wonderful marine mammals safe.

Dolphins are interesting marine mammals. What else do you want to learn about them?

GLOSSARY

adapted (uh-DAPT-ed) Changed to fit new conditions.

blowhole (BLOH-hohl) A nostril opening in the top of the head of some marine mammals, through which they breathe.

blubber (BLUH-ber) The fat of a whale, penguin, or other sea animal.

echoes (EH-kohz) Sounds heard again when they bounce off an object.

echolocation (eh-koh-loh-KAY-shun) A method of locating objects by producing a sound and judging the time is takes the echo to return and the direction from which it returns.

flippers (FLIH-perz) Broad, flat body parts that help animals swim.

flukes (FLOOKS) The two parts of a dolphin's or whale's tail.

juvenile (JOO-vuh-nyl) Relating to young animals.

mammals (MA-mulz) Warm-blooded animals that have a backbone and hair, breathe air, and feed milk to their young.

marine (muh-REEN) Having to do with the sea.

mate (MAYT) To come together to make babies.

performers (per-FAWR-merz) People or animals that put on shows.

pollution (puh-LOO-shun) Manmade waste that harms Earth's air, land, or water.

strand (STRAND) To end up on the land along a body of water and be unable to return to the water.

warm-blooded (WORM-bluh-did) Having a body heat that stays the same, no matter how warm or cold the surroundings are.

WEB SITES

Due to the changing nature of Internet links, PowerKids Press has developed an online list of Web sites related to the subject of this book. This site is updated regularly. Please use this link to access the list:
www.powerkidslinks.com/marm/dolphins/